An effervescent debut, brimming over with novel thoughts, images, and points of view. Held together by an upbeat, pleasing music all the way through.

—**Dave Lordan**, multi-genre writer, performer, editor, and educator

Every so often, a poet reminds us what language can do—Casey's words are so visual that you almost feel helpless as they force you deeper into a world that is gritty and raw. It is unusual to see an emerging voice so stylistically assured. But there is so much more to this collection than its technical accomplishments—Casey's poetry is precisely the kind that Ireland needs right now, full of colour, sex, and bodies. The refrains are ones of experience with which an entire generation will identify.

—**Dr James O'Sullivan**, lecturer, author, publisher

Ingrid Casey's poems are the distilled voices of a mind, spirit and attitude that live within those rare honest poets, seekers, and seers, who are an immediate inspiration to any reader that needs to be moved.

—**Malik Ameer Crumpler**, poet, rapper, curator, editor

In Mandible, *Casey travels through free verse lyricism and spoken word rhyme, Molly Bloom and yoga, jazz and suffragettes, satire of the Kardashians with 'backtalk to/ colonials, old or new'. Her poetry invites us into a new place, where edges intersect . . . We all have to find new mandibles, new ways to eat and speak and offer back what it is we chew on.*

—**Richard Krawiec**, Jacar Press

Fierce and glorious, these empowered songs of womanhood will dazzle you.

—**Kerrie O'Brien**, poet

Ingrid Casey's debut collection Mandible *is visceral, imaginative and sometimes surreal. It charts a tale of a failed relationship and more using mythology, legend and strong images.*

—**Jean O'Brien**, poet

Dear Rose

Mandible

Ingrid Casey

Thanks for coming to my launch!

♡ Ingrid Casey

Ⓟ The Onslaught Press

Published in Oxford by The Onslaught Press
20 March 2018

ISBN: 978-1-912111-56-5

The poems, titles & front cover are set in Jean François Porchez's **Le Monde Livre**,
the back cover and end matter in **Le Monde Sans**

Printed & bound by Lightning Source

for my parents

The point is how to find a use for fury

—*Jo Shapcott*

Whorl

They are listening to the Wu and smoke billows blue,
Fifa greens the screen, the girls are silent, it's Saturday.

Pyramids of Dutch gold. The parents are out visiting, one
silent girl will take his hand, it will be accidental it will

be hybristophilia, they will go to bad planets, there will
be blood on the walls, she will be couched in a glass well,

an obdurate thing, she will smash the ceiling but it will
take years, meanwhile he will see lions and bears with the

pills, she will see tears and doctors and speculums and this
will not be love but a fire pit, a place to grow miracles from dirt.

Milennials

I go to Hades once a month, to check if I'm still
alive. I look up at the roots of the trees; ash, oak,

lyme; these subterranean lungs, broccoli, bronchioles.
There are thirty five nationalities in the incoming class;

gender is fluid, words flow, two and a half
decades cracked open the sternum of this land. This is our island
changing for the better. The salt has fallen out of the

letters, now.   No ripple

of truth, so my liver told, pushed down on solar plexus
every drop of gall incurred, curs, hurls, thighs, cars, boys,

men, schoolyards, stockrooms, shady Shelerin road, places
where gangsters falling made the news, but not the attempt

to rape, to silence me on a post-session Saturday. The tiger's
roar of that decade screamed louder than goodness. I release

the silence, and write; a lustration. I set my daughter's
star on the arc of the roots, the map that will guide her around

this earth's circumference. May she live among trees, overland.

Girl Wor(l)ds

Laughing about uptalk and vocal

fry, I realize, fuck! My soft daughter

is edged with razors. Impersonating

the Kardashians, but shy about showing

it off: she knows, too, satire is mean. Where

are we, us Irish? In the uproar of what is our

long-surrogate tongue. Let her back talk to

                    colonials old or new. Atta girl.

Artemisia

On Sherkin Island, sits at a picnic
table, shelling mussels, atop a hill.

Holes cut in iron that the sun shines
through, spelling her name, the

green and blue, the breeze of it. She
appears to tourists, tells them of the

bitterness in her throat. They pluck
the almonds out for her, once a month

they Heimlich maneuvre her, they
extract milk, they sometimes find raspberry

seeds embedded in her tonsils, they grow
them, return with cakes for her. Once a German,
Judith, found a lump of lead. She drew a woman,

climbed inside, it fit her just fine. You have a
double shadow, that's grief, said Artemisia, let

me rub it out, taking a giant eraser
from her long skirt pockets. Wombs, she said,

the bright bricks the fimbria, are our houses.
Judith told her she was a fencer, and could

easily have cut the shadow. No, no, it's not
about the cutting, it's about the making, it's

not the cutting, or the iron, it's the sun, the
womb, the orbs, that light up my name.

Molly Bloom goes to yoga

Yes I made three hearts, and hinted at one more, no
I don't feel like writing about scourges or gyres or

changes or art because today the writing is about
laminar flow, aquatic claim on phallic, no tumult or

smashing or sloshing but a clear glass, illusive stream,
the knowledge that during savasana there are thousands

of possible hearts skipping about the room, there are hands
touching your hands, the sacred hands the veined vascular

moments of magic the carpet is rough you are supine you
are released you don't need politics or whisky or edgy shit

and you're as much of a poet as Hector or Roland and you
listened to Herbert about always questioning and your clown's

face, you still love makeup but you understand that reality is
the thing we dream into being and truth is a light in the navel.

Kundalini

Night vaults across the
ceiling, out the velux window, a

net, fishladen, stars clinging. What
are you, *undinė* he asks without

article, her fiery fountains, lava, water,
the floor ruined, tiny arks float. Flying

foxes' eyes watch from corners. She's a
cardinal crimson carmine   carpet blushing, flaring under
him. His
mouth, penile pink shocks flowers grow up walls the room
is full and singing. Chakric dots climb connect to elemental

white blue light, his garnet fingers give her back her memory
of joy before life, the flash of zinc that is conception and miniscule

universes and chances and this is the opposite of the abyss zone,
sea coral corrected, shout pops the heart, her hands dig

him, he's mast, rainbow judders up volcanic
spine, burst through, marine snow a crown.

Caravaggio's Eels

Not perciform or anqualee,
their voltage starts low and
blasts out black ghost knife
fish from the blue, vastly and
quick, they attack horses off
Sicilian rocks. One time they
swam cruciform in blood dark
water, a winedark blade sank,
billowed past their lit-fish torsos,
Eyes a-glitter beneath dead stars.

Nobody Can be Atlas

I keep thinking about UA Fanthorpe,
and a suspect edifice held up

in the air
and the beach sky, Wexford. Him
flying a kite, me holding

the babies, sand whipping
us and my fingers

tipping the sky, holding
up the blue sheet of it.

Šartrezas

With a head full of Russian writers, I
asked him to take me inside the onion

dome, after the swimming pool where
I had bobbed like a sponge, my gold

baby dancing inside me, an icon being
painted with each stroke. We were the

last country to be converted, he boasted,
eyes dancing like a goat. We used to sacrifice

virgins, throw them off rocks, collect ferns
during midsummer. While we illumimated

manuscripts and hid from Vikings, I laughed.
I met his eyes then, silent under the heat of a

hairdryer, two dark rebels, irises grew green.

Inside the Beehive, there are no Bruises

There was cheese there, I was the boss. And grapes,
love, alcohol, good manners and blame, a-gently
buzzing. Honey soured slowly, jokes suggestions
admonishing, please don't swear, make me a sand-
wich, and questions and questions and questions are
you sure, *are you sure he cheated*, my sister mother
protectors echoing. When gut is ignored, fear moves
house, into liver, anger a new home. A new home, he
did it all they were so small six months two years not
born. *But we've been through so much.* The nun in re-
hab, charmed, he joined the choir there, he even stole
my hobbies. Teasing, teasing, winching wedge my clever
daughter started to hate, ten year clear eyes stricken. Smell
of it, reverberated off walls talked under my nails, cat on a
ball holding it all, I fell, I fell, what a mess. Scratched at all
but him, his other women even the bookies one day shaking,
shaking at the ballet studio, yer one from his job eyeballing
me from closing corridor walls, and in this way he got me
from all sides, *try not to live your life in hatred* his mother
implored through veils, other languages. Come home then.
I met someone, I'm leaving. His nation, vampires, but I housed
that blood twice, a chimerical comedy. The counsellor, questioning
my repeated use of the word, *stupid, stupid, stupid, stupid*.

Flutter

Storytelling lulls, so he
wraps those lovely arms about

the orb of her,
mammaries, melon.

Fresh fruit swims within,
overripe clings without.

He's mask, mask, mask,
ingesting bounty.

Placing three aggregates, he's calm.
She heaves.

He hands in what, probably thousands.
Cash.

She pushes, bears
down. He's lost; shrivels

fast. Fish baby, melon
surfaces, bobs.

Gleaming.
Chattering, she is equidistant
from fresh and fallen.

The Gambler misses his Mother

He lost his accent in a rush, he lost it in the grounds
of the cathedral, sleeping rough three weeks after he
arrived, he lost it in lines and in the shoes of strippers,
he lost it in the stream of steam as a barista, he lost it in a
machine, on paper slips in the bookies, he lost it in cars,
maternity wards and in the pupils of his sons, those dilating
cameras fixed upon his mark, he lost it in stars seen from
bridges he thought would be the one he'd jump from, he
lost it on the first flight, he lost it at the beach on the run
as a teen, he lost it when his dad left him, he lost it when
he left his sons, he lost it in the pants of all the women he
seduces, he lost it in mirrors, in lakes where his limbs swim
strong, he lost it when they sent him away, he lost it in bottles
at basketball games under beds in sheds, he lost it in every
boat he's fished from, he lost it on canal banks and in the soft
lighting of all the restaurants, he lost it in the tills he steals
from, he lost it in light pockets, he lost it in rehab among
the lushes, he lost it in the rushes of rivers, he lost it while
fucking, he lost it watching porn on his phone every day, he lost
it in churches at meditation, he lost it out running swiftly, he
found it Skyping his mother. He found it during brief weeks
back home, none of his countrymen here can conjure it, only she
holds the key to the box of secrets and memory, the pool in
which the old him swims up to the surface, she's water, she's
giving him life. He's born in her garden, he's normal there, single
weeks at a time. It trips, trails from trouser hems on the return.

After Jazz, some death Tango in the Bathroom

Also possibly on the sofa. Flowers, sprigs,
and a zip on the front of my dress. Hands

enveloped me, delivered me from plane,
hands the size of bell towers on Balearics.

A death dance, winter insects, I cut his clothes,
a telenovela, a thing his mother watched from

eye of pumpkin seed, glass house tomatoes saw
seeds inside me. She knew my eyes, for him, grew

larger than fairy tales, larger than the cellar furnace.
My heart pumped in her ear, red like her

nails. He wrapped me in snow, two sons, one for
each spring, her plums and pears shone. I knew

then, when he held my arms down on hospital beds,
handed me the princes, my body would be an aftershock,

to unravel, winters and winters and winters.

Family Law

At the house, incense fills halls, stairwells, a purge.
Removed, you inhabit this consultation room.

Sequestered, a cobbled corner of Temple Bar, it
is empty but for two chairs; a desk; a dirty window.

Stomach acid echoes the ghouls below; growls at
the spores floating in light. Wait, write,

sit deeper into your life. At the bar, the bibs,
the wigs, wait, write, an act of lavation, make

gold
the air, the words, you are mother,

you are temple, the door opens now,
you are four hearts,

chambers full, a chimera,
sacred.

Access

Opium tea trills your phone, you

can't move every time they are

picked up, shiny cars. You get a

mini fever on Wednesdays; glandular

residue. It's not safe; beats calm, geese

and bow strings rise, fall, the boomerangs

will be delivered to your sick arms at eight.

Families

Today we went all
around follies and corn

fields burnished gold, the
sky sloping towards cicadas, telling

off early-falling helicopters. I met
one of my group, her name had

slipped but she knew me, we did
updates; her son's in New York now,

she bestwished me; we hugged. The
summer looked me straight in the eye,

I could stay in those fields all year, forget
the winters, the tears only come back in the car.

In Malta a Ghost Visits Me

On the balcony, in Mellieha, that
Marian shrine, connected right from

Vilnius to Reykjavik. I sit still, the air
rippled over me like warm water, the wine

swimming around in my veins. It was a woman
relative I'd say, sat across from me, held my skull,

the linen of her hands like hypocephali. My daughter's
life is safe. Imbued, assured, I laughed. It's her birthday.

An Apology to my Daughter

We lived on Avenida de Burjassot near the
Turia, that dried up river bed, snaking
its way through the city. At its tail end by the
port, they were pulling up the Formula One
tracks, and it was the first time I'd been there,
and a dead cock rolled up on shore, a warning
not to love men lacking redemption. We took
buses with our friend from Salamanca to the
Botanical gardens and the museum brimming
with golden icons and ate melon on marbled
floors, godless at twenty five, I took all five
years of you to sit outside the Opera house
at cool fountain spume, watch the guys on
bikes with no saddles. Navigating according
to the bridges, from our first balcony that time
where the flood was, Mestalla stadium was
lit, clouds of fire after matches and you lived
on me like a shell crab, oblivious to my folly.
You crawled over the Gulliver sculpture with
the other children, hot July ants. When you fell
asleep on my lap at the outdoor cinema, I thought
of the few books I'd brought, and Leonard Cohen's
mother asleep came to me, like her you slept through
the crescendoes and anthropomorphic heroes. Anxiety
a red flag to my days, my body browned and shrunken,

we learned the metro stops off by heart
while the men went bouldering under the bridges, amid
street dogs and swathes of joggers and the city was laid
out before us like a beautiful blanket of sand, all stone
and pinking marble and heat. Religious processions walked
between tinfoil and tanned breasts down to bless crosses at
the sea, hooded and pointed and gilded. The cockroaches in
our flat spoke pidgin Spanish to me, told me there were no
school places for you, and I cried when my sister came, and
went, a Madrileño made of cardboard on her arm. Our neighbour
the Colombian though, she made me eat rice and her daughter
and you played, when we danced in her kitchen, we needed no words.

Parents

When you walked the Camino
I remember you came back with a

Mexican amulet and soda bread recipes,
skinny and bearded and blue-eyed as ever.

You and Mam said the twice-blessed voodoo
saved you from that smack on the head in the

hostel shower. You put it in my bag this morning
and took me in your chariot to cross Lethe and speak

my Truth. Ghouls swaggered around, one with a calf
swastika, growling, perfor-

Ming. Dynasties, histories, all forms of Human Life. I
had yellow all around me since yesterday, so I ate a

passionfruit when I came back home, thank you both
for this heart, this stomach not churned.

Mam

And what did you first love?   The colour red.
And who did you first love?   My mother.
The red was her sweater. In pre-language we speak
Colour. She has watched me

    fight, birth, fight, birth,
    myself and others. In the
    beginning we were at War,
    I'd sit on the stairs, waiting,
    rat on her to the demigod.
    I wanted her to play; she was
    hard. I saw glimpses, Hausa
    patterns, love letters in the
    wardrobe, Toulousaine, Maltese
    tan in photos. She can pick grammar
    like fine crochet, I was third so it was
    breezy, Stevie Wonder in utero my first
    ever gig. I loved her Rizzo face, Cleopatra
    brows and nose and loose hands for baking.
    I hated her too, leaving me blind in the face of
    sex, slammed with iron morals, little information,
    my heart clammed, squared against love. But she
                saved me she saved me she learned about red
                in middle age, all the ways to have a daughter.

On Talking to a Humanitarian about Resilience

And what about those
that don't have it, he asks.

I feel the hand of All cup
my jaw, close my mouth.

In this office with two,
all the faces of the

nation past, present,
future; looking up, looking

out from the bookshelves, in-
side air bubbbles trapped in

handles of ceramic cups, in folds
of soggy cardboard in doorways,

for the answer.

Suffragette

ɔme sails a caravel through concrete, savage
ɪt going ninety, past the dog roses and poppies

 glass-littered wasteground. Her dark daughter swinging
n the mast, sails billowing. Jerome's straight brows crooked into a furrow,

's a maidenhead; this morning she awoke, her form changed. A Peregrine
:on, her Da repeated, you're a Peregrine Falcon, love. She'd been on her

ˈ to the Social to tell them about the problem with the silverfish and the damp in
house, and the stopped maintenance. Fear, the demon sitting on

of the fridge, red-veined leathern wings aflap, crackling, cackling. Nah pal, not this
ε, I still have my own human voice, she'd said, looking him in the eye

ɪ ruffling her new feathers. From Corduff right up to the gates of Leinster House,
a ship that had appeared that morning. Just as well, laughed her Da, your NCT

 up on the Micra. Now off you go. The garda eyeballing her. I'm a jigsaw piece,
says to him, frayed and uncomfortable to the Maker, but I do belong here. The

:ton woman rings her from inside the building, her daughter puts the phone on
dspeaker. I can offer you emergency accommodation for a month. In a cage.

Gilgamesh's sister aged 30, on the Pill

Cedar trees ring the ghost estate where Gilgamesh's sister lives. She
came to Blanch when she was ten, nobody could pronounce her name,

her Iraqi eyes silently razing the French teacher to the ground by the
time she was thirteen, the school corridors a swirl of epic Dublin glottal

stops, tongues kept low, a class position of holding in the breath, of holding
in the life, a postcolonial peacetime madness she couldn't comprehend, but

dropped her T's by fifteen, to swim with the shoal. Gilgamesh's sister, does
anyone remember your name? In this sprawl, sunken town, in this vulture

funded house, alone in the galley kitchen the batchelor palette; biscuit, blue,
black. The hand that rocks the clock tells her eyes it's pill time. Her sleeping

son of six months clambers over clouds, out of the golden curled, respiring,
solid limbs, on dreams he flies laughing, away from his young mother, a stone

at the bottom of a teal sea, a broken galleon. Her mind is stretched like hide,
skinning over and around time, the black clouds on her peripheral vision bicker.

Once Upon A Time In Town

The Rabbit up there in IMMA has finally
come to life, had enough of people taking
his picture without consent, the metal of
him lit by the clock at 3.33 am, enlivened,
corporeal. Stepped down into dark sunken
gardens, the chewing gum limbs of him wily
and free, gambolling around sphere trees and
cone plants, espaliered things and boxed tulips.
Wellington glowers from afar, a statue on her plinth
grinding, craning her stony neck to get a goo at him.
A night photographer stands motionless on mezzanine
steps, cigarillo smoke tickles Rabbit's nose. He leaps,
twirls away up to a chestnut tree, fulsome leaves like
hands, conkers now on his rabbit breath, green jacket
jewels. It's rolling in, darkest hour before dawn buzz.
He switches his softening face towards town, coils legs
around, barber pole pattern. Loping, he finds his purpose
in the still waters around the hips of Anna Livia, she takes
his hand, the bean pole and the floozie, it's the greatest love
story ever told. I want my children she says, they spill out
of her hair, they spill out of the Ashling hotel, file after drip-
dripping Plurabelle, mercurial Rabbit. It's late summer the
pub hanging baskets are pink women in labour about to drop
glory. The lovers and and growing rabble of school uniformed
children, pyjama'd children, tae kwon do children, up the Dubs
children, Vote Vote Vote for deValera children, here comes Lisa
at the door children, Queenie-I-Oh children, armbands and Crayola
and very little dóidín suckling children snake their way up past
Moldovan shops and Brazilian bakers, levitate the Luas tracks, they
float over the puke and piss and damp sleeping bags of Henry Street,
oh! Here's Joyce but he stays solid, metal won't budge, cane jaunty.
At a trot now, more children spill out from hotel windows, a mass
of laughter and sand, the merry eyes of them, on down past Cassidys
and Trinity, up to mad Molly and Phil Lynott they'll sing to these children
they'll feed them Dublin Bay prawns they'll cradle them in a wheelbarrow
and rock them back to sleep cockles and mussels and why shouldn't they.

Jazz in a Northern City

Amidst turmoil, paindragon carried me
for nights, to see the Goth. She was in
Macbeth with the artist,
the room was filling with books, miniature

figures, heated exchanges, we rolled downhill,
to the galleries. I filled her ears
with chocolate, she was beaming. Her black Halloween
curls twined around doorways, illustrated our friendship.

There
are silences,
empathy in the space,
in the difference squared

between floor and ceiling.
On this day there
was Sun Ra, at perfect pitches, head
phones suspended in a whole constellation.

The child inside could reach a star, listen. It
was dark,
melodious,
soothing, and definitely
love.

Soma(tic)

Block, block, block, baby's building blocks,
glycerine bubbles drifting silently to the floor,
he was sanguine, did I love him enough, through
the silence, the slant of light in the mornings, did
he know his father was gone? I know I sat with him,
I am afraid, I am afraid that dolor entered him from
me, a channel. But he stood, danced, at seven months.
His tongue is silver, he spoke at ten months, he told clear
stories and songs not long after. His father came, and went,
again. He is a child brimming, steaming with joy, there is
no sadness in me that can stop his soft hyperplastic limbs,
he astounds the dance teacher, his foot extends like my awe,
his grandfather gleeful at his hands' dexterity. I think, I did ok.

He has a brother. Heft, block, strong. I loved him first, it almost
killed my breasts, it almost killed my brain. He sweats, more, he
is so male, taught, anxious, he is his father in miniature. I must
watch him more, love him more, reassure him more. This is what
people mean when they ask about favourites; it is about fear. When
the leavings were, he had already entered the language, and slept
less, so saw more. My guilt is a bird, circling him. I didn't mean to
show him me in distress, the guilt is a double bind. I took him out-
side; in nature, he trusts. I repeated the formula, four years. He writes,
illustrates the monsters, the quests, the heroes. I watch the architecture,
I build painstakingly, a thing I'm not qualified to create, I will not stop.

Arabesque

On the morning of the phlox moon I dreamt of
a pink blood foot, severed, served as breakfast

fare to my children by a faceless man. I ran 1.85
kilometres, motionless on a treadmill. Later I met

my favoutite fop, the psychic one, we talked pressure.
Later I met my pagan friend, helping pilgrims with

migraines. Later I went to get milk and and saw a child
run into the road, barefoot. Women called for authority,

chased the child, wrung hands while men pulled up hoods,
rolled cigarettes, averted eyes. All day this chopped foot

followed me, flopping and dripping and crying pinkly for
me to be like a child, to run free, the women will catch me,

I will catch myself, run, run, run on the earth.

Jubiliejus

I put on the Skeleton Tree,
I painted my bedroom white, it was

the morning it was an exorcism, the
walls were freed my bones matched

all four, it was a meditation it was only
one day, not remarkable, September but

I loved myself then, remembered I'm dead,
eaten clean, dried out in air, hearts' windows open.

Mandible

Draw this beak, this jaw. It can
susurrate, masticate, oscillate, fellate, well
assist with at least. It forms a well-rounded
chin, which you stick out when petulant or
guarded or inquisitive. Never slack, except
for on one side, the left, which betrays your
emotion. Gristle inside, temporomandibular
tantrum. Too much talking, moil in sleep,
lopsided feelings. You need to speak, write,
execute what is inside, balance the blue
throat chakra. When you walk past trees it
relaxes; tightens in the car, under the duress
of traffic and all the spineclimbing aggravations
the stress, the grubwork of teeth, of gears. Lying
on sand can wrap this Hermes-in-the-bones
around on itself. Also hot stones, aromas and
the hands of others sliding along the lines of
para-sympathetic systems, slackening, the
opposite of nervous. Once, a criminal caressed
it, gently and unexpectedly. Out shot colours
from your crown, six or seven weeks. Limning
your outlines, a shaman from the wrong side but
all was yellow then, a clear river. Cock your head
now, cup it in your own hand, remember to choose
to rest. Bird, be free. Sing, speak, sleep.

Martin Heidegger

Has been resurrected, he is now
a piece of origami, a paper bird.

Twenty different sides, one for each
truth. Hanging from a tree in your

garden, he taught us how to fold and
unfold our faces, open to each other like

lily pads on a summer's day.

Ask me how the sky is

In August. Cumulonimbus, cuneiform is
bulbous, ova speak to the sky at summer's death. Running

high on river fever, sex a baptism, step into warms baths, step
into warm hands, step into warm skies, hands write, gather the

letters of limbs, creases, place hot balustrades, almonds on skin.
Mediation, Liffey Swim, my city, Italian quarter, I am pieced

out, chunks like clouds, I am bundled, bunches, stamens, effluvium.

Me and my Friends,
or How to Mend a broken heart

Marigold: from the genus Tagetes. Origin: Tagus, Estruscan god of wisdom

Go see the Elgin marbles, rock robes, draped sentinels. Go have
pizza in Fulham, see monsters in the art section of Harry Potter
world. Don't forget about the man with the rattle
in a football who coaches the blind team; you didn't steal anything.
Look at river glitter, like beads on dresses in the V'n'A, bubble your
way along South Bank with prosecco and menthols, the sun is here.
Talk to a pug at an improv musical in an inflatable purple tent. Watch
seas of orange and crimson turbans and robes spill from
coaches, a Sikh genocide remembered, hearts beating now at Empire's
centre. Subcontinental marigold, a celebration of colour, let it into
your eyes. On the Strand walk with Sligo people, remember how loved
you are. There is a cafe, your lion son's name lettered on it like him, bold
and yellow. At home, walk side by side through avenues, repeat old spells
go to Carmen, rousing and let Rufus piano you, let concert halls push your
heart up out the ceiling. Dance at all the weddings, hot soup pools in Julian
Malta, get your feet in, play badminton in Fairview park, flip flop over
dunes at the Reek, squeal into the wind and at the clouds rolling in to
massage the mountain. Moan on schoolruns with the neighbours, they wined
you too and saved you, they give you tinfoil you give them an onion,
this barter system is called love, your community. With your siblings
at Tara fly kites you're a queen, and these were the happenstances of your
golden grief, it was more like a party. You were wise to keep faith through
that first thin winter London light, God how it hurt your whole body stiff
with it, teeth aching. And after the shock subsides, all this, this healing.

Nicolas Matas

Happy birthday, Nick, you're
twelve today, we miss you in

this house. I remember the
first time we met, before I had

two little boys who look a lot like
you, when you were four. Wax in

your ears was making you cry, I
sat you on my knee and wiped the

tears away, I was already a Mam.
I think about how you ate cornflakes

with yoghurt and your favourite word
in Lithuanian was *plika*. Cycling, Mario

kart, fishing, dirty nails and so shy. In
Loren's house you came home with cat

allergies, punched looking eyes. Finger
dipped pots, you planted seven foot tall

sunflower seeds with me. I hope you grow
like that, I hope you shine. You are still loved.

Love: After Neruda's Sonnet XXXIII

Florica walks behind Inspector, to home where she's not
at-home. Children's eyes and begonias meet
her here, on this threshold, waiting
for her to give them chocolate, water.

Her crushed velvet skirts have followed
his silver through tracts, across karst; Carpathia, Kiev,
Berlin. Now here, to eternal damp and clouded
summers and loved masonry.

He sees the amber of the sun
in her kitchen eyes at day's end; she's
a building that flies without buttress.

He lets her make coffee and listens
to her laugh peal in time with the
boiling water, bells in unison.

Samhain

On the Wednesday before Samhain, I am making
a typo in the IM to my besto about the summer of
1816, the summer of no sun, I say summer of no sin,
is there such a thing, we emojicate, jocular, of course
not, but Shelley's summer, as I'd been reading over the
clouds of gothic steam rising from Wednesday kitchen
mince being garlicked to within an inch of its life, as I
run to the neighbours for a tin opener, that summer was
biblical, umbilical, brown snow fell on Hungarian fields
while Byron and company settled around other mountains,
moved enough to create monsters out of the mahogany, the
terrible summer skies. What sin, to birth such a monster. I hear
the children clamouring, crashing into this, my realm, my radio
moments, my online journal and fleeting chats moments, I lay out
the knives, the pumpkins will be carved and we will read stories during
Samhain and nine months later we will sin, every summer, we will
birth storm stories.

Glock

We stood, arms
linked, facing on a fallen tree. Old

words printed inside crowns. The shot
came then; you stumbled back, shame a

soft-needled bed. I stepped off at the end, five
or maybe seven steps later. You'd composed need;

drew me to you. Sentinel acting out love, a post-fact,
hard, liar, perfectly velvet in the greening air.

Rasputin in Dublin 15

He's a mad bastard, he lives on a traffic island opposite
the Lithuanian shop there in Blanchardstown. You already
know exactly what he looks like; wax trenchcoat, old white Huaraches
laced up to cut off blood. He fell out of an aristocrats river, he was
reincarnated as a gypsy and now he's an alcoholic. Rasputin! Look
at the hack of you, plastic rosary beads around your neck, coffee cup
begging, trying to wash car windows, your beard a greasy bib. There's
a demon on each of your shoulders, angry bulbous leather little yokes,
they try to eat the flies circling your head. Aneta Valova, the owner of
the launderette, does be having none of you. Shoo! She actually said last
week, the wagon, when you tried to beckon over her chihuahua, Pixie.
The weekend teenage bus stop boys call the dog Poxy, they think you're deadly,
and give you vodka that makes you see the road as an eel, a strip of the old world.
One time two of the Nigerian girls on their way home from school cut through
the tunnels and ran straight into you, on your way back from a root around the
hospital grounds. Papa Legba, they called you, screaming blue murder, and it's
true you were standing at the T junction cos a 39 bus was trundling by, full of
college students, affluents, accents that don't see you. They can't; only the new,
the strangers and underdogs do.

Vigile

In the shower, the fireman marvels at the grit under his nails.
At night, he chokes in his sleep. After six months of roaring
about Hercules and giants in the dark, the fireman's girlfriend
decided that enough was enough. She loved, of course, to watch
his brow move with the rhythm of her breath, his drool like dew
on her poppies, pomegranate-bead nipples. With the shift work his
sleep patterns danced like loosed marbles, rolling and erratic. The
clinician diagnosed exploding head syndrome and sleep paralysis,
the latter being when the black thing occasionally sat on his chest,
a river he couldn't hold. And his mouth, despite herbal remedies,
yoga and meditation, continued to spit the silt of the Sarno delta. Six
weeks later he was waking up to mouthfuls of ash, foreskin and eardrums
all soot, his hair and lashes peppered with some haunting not of his choosing.

The Boxer Reads To Me

Sit here, I dare you, again for
Sakhalin, salon moments, pore

over the Poet, crease of hip cut
before me like diamonds, spine

coilsprung to recite. Talk to me
about la Motta, the animal, warm

bright rocks on me the primal the
literary ones, you are coal walls

lit up, it's dark, I'm awake with you.

On the Hypnologic

Pomegranates, halved on the plate,
and the table looks like a Dutch master's,

dig the jewels out, pop skin, ruby teeth,
beads, broken necklaces, pearl's blood. Today

was filled with Lucien's peach and green faces,
week old love, the tooth in a ruby. Satiated by

fruit, sweet new things, head nods. Somnolence
makes a dreaming Dali wife of you, tigers, pomegranates.

Synaesthesia In The Guggenheim

Is a dance. Neurons fire, a Catherine wheel

ascends smooth slope, the building a nutshell,

a chrysalis, a cask. Oils and umbers and fruits

lift yellow raincoat right into space at the Monet

triptych, crescendo lilacs eyes, suspends tongues,

arms lift into greens, blues nape of neck, toes are

pinked and there is no time there is only art, now.

A Sonnet with an added Couplet

My notebooks are like lovers; uncostly, fake, easy
to come by. Harder to convey to, whispering
ideas that come to me while bathing, where water
runs off breasts, past rogue coins greened by children,

pooling into obsidian plughole. I stub my toe there, think
about the scars I wanted to show on the day we met. Look,
wrapping my eyes around your teeth, this water is
spooling down ear lobes ready to catch

your breath. See the ways my skin can fail, yet
hold me. I have been waiting for love these three
cheap years, I let my blood with the moons and now

I plush, pluck, knead my rolls, places and musculature.
Can you hear soft thighs speak, can you hear pink of lip
dun of freckle can you see the letters, the words rushing

like water I am clean, I am clean.
Touch me, touch me I am clean.

Atheism is Tinder

How big is your gratitude? As big as

the mountains. Where is your faith?

Stolen. Where's your rage? In the lava.

Do you come? Like the sea. Like rivers.

Who loves you? Nobody, nobody, nobody.

What's the refrain?
A resounding

are you fucking kidding me are you fucking kidding me are you fucking kidding me

Dublin, 2016

Start with Leonardo. The paper has crossed
time and space, for your eyes, just as they are now. There

are hearts as seeds, livers as roots bursting at a perfect pitch of
wild, with June's flowers cheering you on. Caravaggio

brings you home. How long has it been? The light on metal,
hypermasculine guards, buttocks striped silk. This is how the

world was and is; an autoportrait in the background holding up
a light up to betrayal. Walk further into your land, through the

impasto rooms and the horses of the Poet's brother and the pinker
skies, Connemara, the so-big clouds that you know better having

been there in the rosy air. In these cycles and revolutions and gold
leaf wars, art brings you to love.

Why

talk about your kitchen
so much? I'm in there alot.

Today there's a spot on the
wall on the celery salt green

wall it's lit up by winter sliver
was it like this in the tombs in

the passages, my space here is
a galley style it's a corridor so

the sun falls on the dining wall
on the moss wall so I roll my mind

around the vowels of it I roll my eye

closer to the window to the light there

will not be much more darkness, in
November crypts were light smooth

and sand, Césaire was there, palms
under porticos and floating gold. What is

this black floored ordinary set of tiles and
cupboards but a lesson in immensity, in

cities and how to grow healthier moulds.

Natural Born Producer

You cannot shame the winter politico
he cares not for Loach or tins of beans

or snow or hair falling out in clumps he
is heart, darkened. Instead let us shine

light onto ourselves, let us gather the anger
and the power and hold it up to him in

ritual in film in online petition this is where
we live now let us amass our

faith in change it will take long days of
patience and labour and phonecalls and

meetings and requests and locations and
stunning favours, it will take several

stumbles and cries but hold this bird this
frail thing it is singing look, the buds are

already rolled ready, be obstinate and grumpy
as a season, predictable and miraculous enough

to effect to effect to effect drop like hail, sting, sing
and unfurl soon, soon green will come back,

be autochthonous be brave always, look at the sky.

To My Younger Son, On His Fourth Birthday

From a winedark table I see a still-bald tree top, a lung.
Snakes and Ladders and your many cards, my fifty

seven month companion. I had thought, during the
labouring, that I was going away from the world,

leaving your siblings. You made a star of me in that
triangle, the consultant at my back, your father's arms

the masts I clung to, and I a ship in full sail. Up from
the hold you came, all vernix and April fury. But there

has been no betrayal, and I am no ship. We are on land,
another branch; you grow carefree, shuck off rain, snow,

and we are fractal, we are fractal, we are four years fractal.

Meditation

Listen to the evening come down. Boot clicks, gravel-

rumble under the thud-thud of a leather ball. Gladioli

curls, loll on indigo fur, lamps are lit. Kids called home,

names like Evan distill the darkening air. Eavan on your

mind; this satellite village is safe, the house a capsule. Sedate;

a womb of one's own. Float, you're a paper cutout, earth, water

and sky. A part of this tableaux, be still. You're home.

Notes

Whorl: The Wu refers to a high-profile American hip hop group from the 1990s.

Artemisia: Artemisia Gentileschi was the daughter of Ovidius, contemporary of Caravaggio. Accepted by the Academy in Florence, she was a rape survivor and vindicated in court, and became financially successful in middle age due to her artistic talent. There is a metal sign bearing her name outside the Jolly Roger pub on Sherkin Island, off West Cork. Judith in the poem refers to Judith slaying Holofernes in one of Artemisia's paintings.

Molly Bloom: Herbert here refers to Zbigniew Herbert, a Polish poet who talks about looking at 'your clown's face' in his amazing poem, The Envoy of Mr. Cogito, that warning to Europe. The poem is about taking responsibility, and in doing so, being mindful, and allowing joy in.

Kundalini: undinė; Lithuanian for mermaid.

Nobody Can be Atlas: references UA Fanthorpe's beautiful poem, 'Atlas'.

In Malta A Ghost Visits Me: hypocephali refers to the discs placed under the heads of the dead in ancient Egypt; usually stuccoed linen, papyrus, bronze, gold, wood or clay.

Suffragette: for Erica Fleming, and all the single mothers.

Gilgamesh's Sister: references an epic akin to Homer's *Odyssey*; the earlier Sumerian/Akkadian epic of Gilamesh, set in and around the city of Ur, in modern day Iraq. Loosely based on an influx of immigrants from Bosnia to Ireland during my childhood, and my own experience with postpartum depression. It reimagines how women go on these epic journeys in youth and throughout adulthood, fighting monsters and how that goes mostly unrecorded or not witnessed.

Mandible: the lower jaw bone.

Love, After Neruda's Sonnet XXXIII: In Neruda's thirthy-third sonnet (from *Cien Sonetos de Amor*) he talks about coming home from Armenia, Ceylon; the Yang-Tse. I love particularly the quatrain-tercet form, so I wanted to make a version about Roma nomads in Ireland, neighbours that I see all the time. I reimagined a girl's life, one sent begging at Aldi. In his final tercet, Neruda says that 'love cannot fly without resting' and in this poem I wanted to give this tired girl rest, and romance.

Samhain: About the summer of 1816, known as the 'year without a summer'. An anomalous weather event, due to volcanic ash accumulating in the skies from an eruption at Mount Tambora in the Indian Ocean a year prior. The overcast Swiss skies inspired Shelley's composition of Frankenstein.

The Boxer Reads To Me: Sakhalin refers to an island visited by Chekhov while documenting prison conditions in Siberia, as documented in a great poem by Séamus Heaney (from the collection *Station Island*). In the line about diamonds in Heaney's poem, I have created a volta, whereby the boxer's body is surveyed by the female gaze.

On the Hypnologic: Composed after visiting the Lucien Freud exhibition in IMMA. Dali's wife is referenced here, as depicted in his painting Dream Caused by the Flight of a Bee around a Pomegranate a Second before Waking, and Freudian influences on his surrealist art.

Why: Aimé Césaire's tomb is referenced here, as seen in the Panthéon, Paris. Newgrange, as passage tomb, is also referenced.

Meditation: Eavan Boland's 'This Moment' is evoked here, for the purpose of illustrating how neighbourhoods are crucial to human survival; a moment is taken, to take stock of having survived potential homelessness, and how, in the wake of that experience, Boland's poem, so familiar from the state exams, took on huge new poignancy.

Thanks and Acknowledgements

I would like to thank the following publications, for previously featuring some of the work in this collection: *The Moth magazine*, *The Lonely Crowd*, *The Honest Ulsterman*, *Southword*, *Poethead*, *The Stony Thursday Book*, *A New Ulster*, *The Interpreter's House*, *Banshee magazine*, the Three Drops Press, the *Looking At The Stars* anthology, *The Opiate*, and *Spontaneity*, *Visual Verse*, and the *Winter Solstice* anthology.

I would like to thank Alice Kinsella, Kerrie O'Brien, Colm Keegan, David Hynes, Jessica Traynor, Paul Casey and Dr Declan Kavanagh for their support along the way, their friendship and inclusion. Thank you to Mathew Staunton and everyone at The Onslaught Press for choosing and putting this book together, and thank you to Conor Horgan for the cover photograph.

Thank you to my parents, and Elise, Leon and Kajus. Thanks to my siblings, friends and neighbours for always being there too.

Other Onslaught Press Poetry Titles